Fact Finders™

Biographies

Langston Hughes

Great American Writer

by B. A. Hoena

Consultant:
Christopher C. De Santis
Associate Professor of African-American and American Literature
Department of English
Illinois State University
Normal, Illinois

Capstone *press*

Mankato, Minnesota

Fact Finders is published by Capstone Press,
151 Good Counsel Drive, P.O. Box 669, Mankato, Minnesota 56002.
www.capstonepress.com

Library of Congress Cataloging-in-Publication Data
Hoena, B. A.
     Langston Hughes: great American writer / by B. A. Hoena.
     p. cm.—(Fact finders. Biographies)
     Includes bibliographical references and index.
     ISBN 0-7368-3745-0 (hardcover)
     1. Hughes, Langston, 1902–1967—Juvenile literature. 2. Poets, American—20th
century—Biography—Juvenile literature. 3. African American poets—Biography—Juvenile
literature. I. Title. II. Series.
PS3515.U274Z6635 2005
818'.5209—dc22   2004011301

Summary: An introduction to the life of African American writer Langston Hughes,
     who shared his feelings about racism through his work.

Editorial Credits
Megan Schoeneberger, editor; Juliette Peters, set designer; Patrick D. Dentinger, book
     designer and illustrator; Kelly Garvin, photo researcher; Scott Thoms, photo editor

Photo Credits
Corbis, cover; Hulton-Deutsch Collection, 23
Getty Images Inc./Hulton Archive, 1, 27
Yale Collection of American Literature, Beinecke Rare Book and Manuscript Library,
     5, 7, 8, 9, 10, 11, 13, 15, 17, 18, 19, 20–21, 22, 25, 26

Photos reprinted by permission of Harold Ober Associates Incorporated Copyright 2005

1 2 3 4 5 6 10 09 08 07 06 05

Table of Contents

Chapter 1

Rivers

In the summer of 1920, Langston Hughes got on a train in Cleveland, Ohio. He was headed to Mexico to ask his father for money for college.

As the train crossed the Mississippi River, the sunset spread golden light on the water. Hughes imagined that the souls of African Americans were like great old rivers. He began to write.

Hughes titled his poem, "The Negro Speaks of Rivers." In 1921, it was **published** in *Crisis* magazine by the National Association for the Advancement of Colored People (NAACP). The poem was his first nationally recognized poem. Editors at *Crisis* asked him to write more.

I've known rivers:
I've known rivers ancient as the world
and older than the flow of human blood
In human veins!

My soul has grown deep like the rivers.

I bathed in the Euphrates when dawns
were young.
I built my hut beside the Congo and
it lulled me to sleep.
I looked upon the Nile and raised the
pyramids above it.
I heard the singing of the Mississippi
when Abe Lincoln went down
to New Orleans,
and I've seen its muddy bosom
turn all golden in the sunset.

I've known rivers:
ancient, dusky rivers.

My soul has grown deep
like the rivers.

From memory to read
on radio show —
Langston Hughes

Hughes handwrote this copy of
"The Negro Speaks of Rivers" before
reading the poem on a radio show.

Chapter 2

Beginnings

James Langston Hughes was born February 1, 1902, in Joplin, Missouri. His parents were James Nathaniel Hughes and Carrie Langston Hughes. Most people called Hughes by his middle name, Langston.

Hughes' father left the family and moved to Mexico shortly after Hughes was born. James Hughes believed African Americans were treated unfairly in the United States. They couldn't get good jobs or own land. In Mexico, James Hughes became a successful business owner.

A photograph from 1902 shows Hughes with his mother.

Moving Around

After James Hughes left, Hughes' mother had to find work. She often moved to different cities looking for jobs. She could not always take Hughes with her.

Hughes, shown here in 1905, spent most of his childhood with his grandmother.

Hughes' mother left him in Lawrence, Kansas, with his grandmother, Mary Langston. Hughes learned to be proud of his race from his grandmother.

Hughes' grandmother had been part of the abolitionist movement to end slavery. She told Hughes how African Americans had suffered as slaves. She also taught him about Sojourner Truth and other African American heroes.

Hughes' grandmother was a strong woman who believed in equal rights for all races.

9

In 1915, when Hughes was 13, his grandmother died. Hughes moved to Lincoln, Illinois, to live with his mother. She had remarried. Hughes now had a stepfather and stepbrother.

Class Poet

Hughes made many friends at his school in Lincoln. They chose him to be the class poet. He wrote his first poem for his 8th grade graduation.

Hughes posed for this photograph in 1916.
◀ By this time, he was living in Lincoln, Illinois.

In 1916, Hughes and his family moved to Cleveland, Ohio. Hughes went to Central High School. He began to offer his poems and stories to the school's magazine. His writing appeared almost every month.

Hughes (left) had many friends at Central High School in Cleveland. ➡

QUOTE

"I didn't think about being a writer ever. I thought I might like to be a doctor, you know, or else a streetcar conductor . . ."
—Langston Hughes

Chapter 3

Becoming a Writer

After graduating from high school, Hughes hoped to go to Columbia University in New York City. But he didn't have money. In the summer of 1920, he went to Mexico to see his father.

Hughes' father wouldn't help. Without money for school, Hughes stayed in Mexico. He taught English and wrote. Hughes also published poems and **essays** in U.S. magazines. In 1921, Hughes' father agreed to pay for one year at Columbia because of Hughes' success.

As a young man, Hughes decided he wanted to be a writer.

New York and the Blues

In September 1921, Hughes began classes at Columbia. But he didn't like the school. Most of his classmates were white. Hughes felt separated from other African Americans. He decided not to return for a second year.

Many African Americans lived in the Harlem area of New York City. Hughes and other African Americans wrote many works. They became part of the Harlem **Renaissance**, a time in the 1920s and 1930s when African American writing became more respected.

Hughes had difficulty finding work. Jobs open to African Americans did not pay well. In 1923, Hughes got a job on a ship headed for Africa. Later, he sailed to Europe.

Hughes often wrote poems about the struggles of African Americans. His favorite style of poetry was the blues. Traditional African American blues are songs about not having money, friends, or love. Most blues are sad, but many also show a sense of humor. Hughes's first book, *The Weary Blues*, included many blues poems. It was published in 1926.

FACT!

Hughes brought home a pet monkey named Jocko when he returned from Africa. The monkey was a gift for his family.

In 1925, Hughes had a job clearing tables in a restaurant in Washington, D.C. ◆

Chapter 4

Poems, Books, and Plays

Hughes continued his education and writing. In 1926, he started classes at Lincoln University near Philadelphia, Pennsylvania. In 1927, he published his second book of poems, *Fine Clothes to the Jew*.

Hughes liked to share his poetry with people. He read his poetry in Harlem and traveled to other towns for poetry readings. He visited southern states to share his poems with African American and white audiences. Many of his poems appeared in magazines.

Hughes posed with his mother after graduating from Lincoln University in 1929.

Not without Laughter was
▼ Hughes' first novel.

The 1930s

Hughes kept writing after college. In 1930, he published his first **novel**, *Not without Laughter*. This book told about an African American family in Kansas. In 1934, Hughes published a book of short stories titled *The Ways of White Folks*.

Hughes also wrote many plays. In 1935, his play *Mulatto* opened in New York. It was performed 373 times before it closed. In 1936, *Little Ham* was performed in Cleveland.

During this time, Hughes traveled a great deal. In 1932, he went to the Soviet Union for a year. He saw how the Soviet Union was run. The country was poor, but it gave free education and health care to all people. Hughes saw no signs of racism. In 1937, Hughes spent several months in Madrid, Spain. He reported on the Spanish Civil War (1936–1939). In his writing, he praised the Soviet Union and Spain's freedom fighters.

▲ Hughes often traveled to give speeches and read poems. Here, he is shown on a trip to Hawaii in 1933.

Chapter 5

A Writing Career

Writing was not an easy way for Hughes to earn money. His poems and plays made some people angry. Hughes dealt honestly with difficult issues, such as racism and poverty. Some people wanted to avoid those issues. Many of Hughes' books did not sell well. Hughes was poor most of his life.

Still, Hughes wrote a great deal. In 1940, he published his **autobiography**, *The Big Sea*. In 1942, Hughes published *Shakespeare in Harlem*. This book included more blues poems. He also wrote poems influenced by African American religious songs, or spirituals.

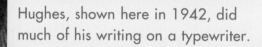

Hughes, shown here in 1942, did much of his writing on a typewriter.

Harlem

Good morning, Daddy!
I was born here, he said,
and I've watched Harlem grow,
(colored folks)
until we spread
from river to river,
all across the island, *middle of the*
I've watched us spread.
out of Penn Station
a new nation,
out of planes from Porto Rico,
the holes
of boats (from Cuba,) chico,
(Jamaica, Haiti,) Panama,
out of busses from Georgia,
Florida, Louisiana, *marked NEW YORK—*
to Harlem, Brooklyn, Bronx, San Juan Hill,
but most of all to Harlem:
montage of a dream deferred,
Tomorrow, ain't you heard?

3 #   # 3

Simple Writing

Hughes wrote a weekly **column** for the *Chicago Defender* newspaper. In 1943, he made up a character called Jesse B. Simple. The character was a young African American man whose wisdom was far from simple. In his stories about Simple, Hughes wrote about everyday difficulties facing African Americans.

▲ Hughes was often not happy with the first copies of his poems. He made notes of changes he wanted to make.

Musicals and Operas

Hughes also worked on **operas** and musicals. He wrote the **lyrics** for *Street Scene*. In 1947, this opera opened in New York and did well. By 1948, Hughes had enough money to buy a home in Harlem. It was the first and only home he ever owned.

In 1957, Hughes finished writing the lyrics and text for *Simply Heavenly*. This musical was based on Hughes' character Simple. It was performed in New York, Europe, and Washington, D.C.

⬆ Actors rehearse for a London performance of *Simply Heavenly* in 1958.

FACT!

Hughes was not a morning person. He usually went to bed at dawn and slept until noon.

Chapter 6

The Last Page

Hughes continued writing and publishing. He wrote several children's books about jazz and Africa. He also wrote a history of the NAACP for adults.

In 1967, Hughes went to the hospital. He was suffering from stomach pain. On May 22, Hughes died after stomach surgery. He was 65.

Lasting Influence

Hughes wrote a great deal during his life. He wrote 15 books of poetry and more than 60 plays. He also wrote many short stories, novels, song lyrics, and essays. Much of his work dealt with struggles and triumphs of African Americans.

Hughes stands in front of his house in Harlem in 1962.

Hughes wrote about what he knew. He wrote about his jobs and travels. He wrote about his family and friends. Hughes showed that poetry was a way for people to share their troubles.

Hughes used his success to help other writers. He visited other countries to talk to writers. He traveled around the United States reading his poems and talking about writing. He encouraged people of all races to use poetry to express the struggles in their lives. Today, Hughes continues to be one of the most popular of all American poets.

Hughes stands with poet Gwendolyn Brooks. Hughes encouraged Brooks to write poetry. She became the first African American to win the Pulitzer Prize.

Fast Facts

Full name: James Langston Hughes

Birth: February 1, 1902

Death: May 22, 1967

Hometown: born in Joplin, Missouri; raised in
Lawrence, Kansas

Parents: James Nathaniel Hughes and
Carrie Langston Hughes

Education: Graduated from high school in 1920; graduated
from Lincoln University in 1929

Major works:

The Weary Blues, 1926

Not without Laughter, 1930

The Ways of White Folks, 1934

Little Ham, 1936

The Big Sea: An Autobiography, 1940

Shakespeare in Harlem, 1942

Simple Speaks His Mind, 1950

Simply Heavenly, 1957

Time Line

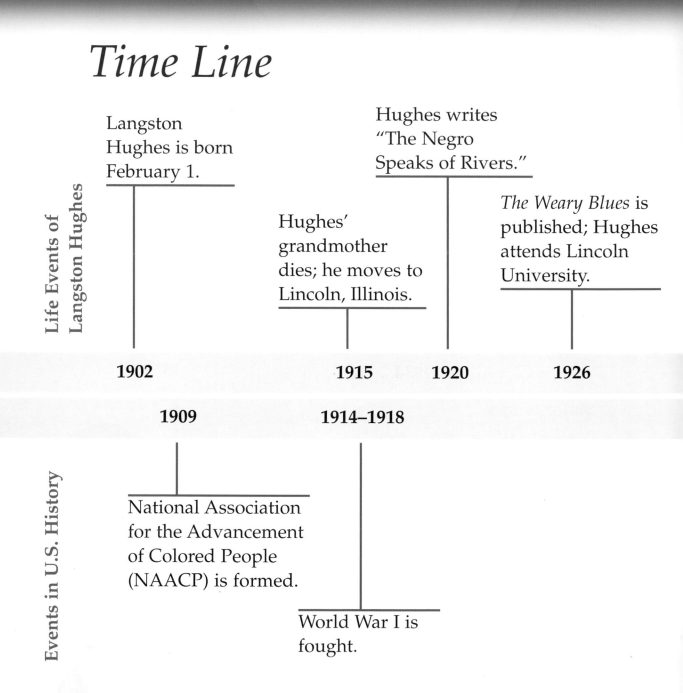

Life Events of Langston Hughes

Langston Hughes is born February 1.

Hughes' grandmother dies; he moves to Lincoln, Illinois.

Hughes writes "The Negro Speaks of Rivers."

The Weary Blues is published; Hughes attends Lincoln University.

1902   **1915**   **1920**   **1926**

1909   **1914–1918**

Events in U.S. History

National Association for the Advancement of Colored People (NAACP) is formed.

World War I is fought.

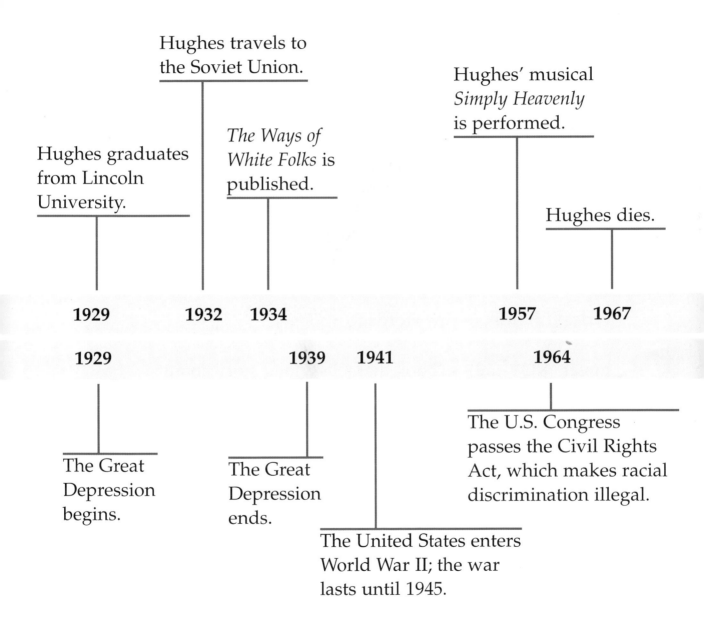

Hughes travels to the Soviet Union.

Hughes' musical *Simply Heavenly* is performed.

Hughes graduates from Lincoln University.

The Ways of White Folks is published.

Hughes dies.

1929   1932   1934   1957   1967

1929   1939   1941   1964

The Great Depression begins.

The Great Depression ends.

The United States enters World War II; the war lasts until 1945.

The U.S. Congress passes the Civil Rights Act, which makes racial discrimination illegal.

Glossary

autobiography (aw-toh-bye-OG-ruh-fee)—a book in which the author tells about his or her life

column (KOL-uhm)—a piece of writing by the same person, or on the same subject, that appears regularly in a newspaper or a magazine

essay (ESS-ay)—a piece of writing that gives the author's opinion on a particular subject

lyrics (LIHR-iks)—the words to a song

novel (NOV-uhl)—a book that tells a long story about made-up people and events

opera (OP-ur-uh)—a play in which the words are sung

publish (PUHB-lish)—to produce and distribute a book, magazine, newspaper, or any other printed material so that people can buy it

renaissance (REN-uh-sahnss)—a period of time when many new works of literature and art are produced

Internet Sites

FactHound offers a safe, fun way to find Internet sites related to this book. All of the sites on FactHound have been researched by our staff.

Here's how:

1. Visit *www.facthound.com*
2. Type in this special code **0736837450** for age-appropriate sites. Or enter a search word related to this book for a more general search.
3. Click on the **Fetch It** button.

FactHound will fetch the best sites for you!

Read More

Burleigh, Robert. *Langston's Train Ride*. New York: Orchard Books, 2004.

Raatma, Lucia. *Langston Hughes: African-American Poet*. Journey to Freedom. Chanhassen, Minn: Child's World, 2003.

Walker, Alice. *Langston Hughes: American Poet*. New York: Amistad, 2002.

Index